Verses for the Violet hour

Arya Sathyan

WRITERS' READERS

Published by Booksthakam, India
info@booksthakam.com
www.booksthakam.com

Verses for the Violet hour

A Booksthakam Book/ published by arrangement with the author

ISBN: 978-93-94378-31-5

Typeset and Cover Design by Cogitabund LLP
Printed and bounded in India by Manipal Technologies Limited

FSC www.fsc.org MIX Paper | Supporting responsible forestry FSC® C043100

CONTENTS

To Pappa

ACKNOWLEDGEMENT

To you, my dearest Pappa, though you passed before I could show you my works, I always carry you in my heart. Thank you for always being the best father that I could ask for and more. You understood me even in my silence and loved me endlessly. Here, I dedicate the apostrophes written in your absence embodying my heart and inestimable gratitude for you.

To my loveliest Mummy, thank you for your unconditional love and unwavering confidence in me. This wouldn't have been possible without your support that has engulfed me like a warm hug in my toughest times. Love you forevermore.

To my sister, Ponnu didi, thank you for having my back, for looking out for me and listening to me rant about random stuff without ever complaining. Thank you for loving me the way you do. Thank you, my second mummy.

To my brother-in-law, Manish bhaiya, even though we're not related by blood, you are nothing short of a real brother. Thank you for your love, all your teasing and inputs. I'm glad to have someone like you.

To Prasad uncle, words cannot describe how I grateful I am for your presence in my life. You have listened to me patiently and offered me solace in my darkest times. You've been with me through thick and thin and your support and belief in me is what keeps me going. I will forever be indebted to you. Nothing in my vocabulary could appreciate your support enough.

Booksthakam Publishers, thank you for believing in me and for giving me a space to grow. Without your dedicated team, this work would have never come to fruition. Thank you for accompanying me in this creative odyssey. Thank you Jefin for introducing me to Booksthakam Publishers. If it wasn't for you, I may have never reached this stage. Much obliged.

Thank you, Adithya Ramesh, Lasya, Amal S, Rishi, Arsha, Dafrin and Gauri Manoj for lending your time to read and voice your inputs. All of your words of appreciation and love means the world to me. Your constant encouragement pushed me to write more and better.

Thank you Maalavika ma'am, Aswathy ma'am and Ramya ma'am for your continuous words of affirmation and feedbacks. It is under your guidance and mentorship that I became confident in my writing and was able to transform my dream into reality. Thank you so much for your time and effort and most importantly thank you for having faith in me. Thank you to all my teachers at Ivanios for sharing with me your unique insights about the world, helping me shape my own perspective. Thank you, Sushil Sir, for your wisdom and for making me view and enjoy poetry in a different light.

And last but not least, thank you, Shobhin Thomas Saj, my muse, for just existing and being yourself. This work wouldn't have been possible if you didn't dominate my stream of consciousness like the way you do. Thank you for evoking a myriad of emotions in me that inspired the poems in this work.

With love,
Arya Sathyan

Verses for the Violet hour

THE EMBRACE

The labyrinth of grim thoughts in my mind's maze
encumbers my fatigued form,
flushed and fevered;
lying on a bed that feels more harsh than comforting,
surrounded by a wasteland of inhuman ignorance and of scarcity of solicitude;
draining all life,
Leaving my dwindling heart despondent.

Until you, my Mother,
'tis in your embrace I hear the rhythmic beating of your heart,
echoing in my ears;
An embrace that engulfs like a warm quilt breathing life into my lifelessness.

THE WAIT

I waited, waited, waited,
For your arms
to embrace me,
To pull me close to your chest
and warm me
like the smooth summer evenings.

I waited for your loving caress
along my tender thighs,
to feel the elated euphoria
blooming within,
like the flowers on a sightly spring.

I waited for your kisses
all over the contours of my face,
to calm me like a zephyr
on a serene winter aurora.

I waited,
smiling wistfully,
for my long lost love.

LOVE IN A STREAM OF CONSCIOUSNESS

My line of vision is crystal clear
as I float in a stream of consciousness,
A wide array of thoughts fleeting,
traversing from non-linear to nonsensical,
A babel of voices in a chaotic chasm.

But when in love,
The anarchy is gentrified.
I no longer float in a stream of consciousness
as your velvety voice steers this stream
into the expansive ocean of your memories.
The maelstrom of thoughts vanish;
Linearity and sense established,
Mind securing a structure
until it becomes an abstract of you.

Now my line of vision is clouded
as the world around fades like an apparition.

HEART TO HEART

Watching the waning moon on a quiet night,
I asked my Father;
"How much do you love me?"
My ingenuous little self
anticipated an answer
based on a scale;
Like from the cavernous oceans to the ether above,
Or till the dying of the observable universe,
Or till time exists,
Instead, he smiled playfully and said,
"I love you from my heart to your heart."
I grinned back like a Cheshire cat,
Sensing the significance of such a statement.

THE CONTRITE LAPSE

A man and a damsel
On a clandestine rendezvous
With desires eclipsing all ethics
Only for the rue to ensue.

INFIDELITY

Losing you was inevitable,
But not expected as soon as now.
From seeing in secret to separating as strangers,
All transpiring in the twinkling of an eye.

We both had headed down the same primrose path;
Both of us knowing it was scandalous.

Yet, you came out unscathed,
Whilst I was condemned wanton and promiscuous.

You were condoned and you moved on with your life,
Whereas I was left alone with all the blame,
And the nauseous guilt rising from my gut,
up towards my bosom;
tormenting my already shattered heart.

Nevertheless, you became the only man in my life;
While I, the other woman in yours.

FALLING FOR FALLACY

His eyes were scintillating
and it blinded her
as she felt amatory love
flourish deep within her.
He gave her the attention
she craved vehemently.
His desire for her flesh
disguised as devotion,
All his chicanery was candour to her.
The dewy-eyed girl
fell into his lecherous trap,
Her gullible goodwill
reluctant to believe
that she was being used,
that she was being devoured
slowly by the Devil.

UNDER THE VINES

Under the vines,
His coquettish eyes
Undress her with fiery fervour,
Hands tracing her curves and lines,
Eager to devour.

Under the vines,
She responds in kind,
Pressing her voluptuous body
against his studly one,
Relishing his arousal.

Under the vines,
He kisses her hard and soft,
A requiem of lost innocence,
Gripping the supple skin of her waist.

Under the vines,
With a sultry gaze,
He mouths the flesh of her chest,
Feeding on to her zest,
Leaving her in a drunken daze.

Under the vines,
They kiss and touch heavily,
And savour the flavour
of their carnal desires.
He tears her asunder,
and she's down to her seductive surrender.
They indulge ardently
in their furtive amour.

Above the vines,
The venereal God Eros,
leers upon them,
Impish, he wallows in being the voyeur.

VANQUISHED LOVE

Against a wall,
I followed the mellifluous resonance
of your yearning unsaid;
As you became the Pyramus to my Thisbe.

Sundered by a wall
of all social constructs,
constraining and conspiring
against our age and contrasts.
Yet we loved,
amidst the hindrance of established ethics
and of both our wedlock's vexations.

But the obligatory obstacle,
much stronger and sonorous
split us apart;
leaving lost love unrequited.

THE AGONY OF A VOYEUR

He watches the kid
who lost his father,
feeling the familiarity.
He watches the woman he loves
from a distance,
Because he doesn't know
how to approach her.
He watches his only friend
in life support,
feeling regretful for not spending
enough time with him.
He watches his world fall apart
in front of his eyes,
feeling the fear of being left alone
in the oblivion.
Unable to bond
with those around him,
He silently watches,
Because that's all
he has ever known in his life.

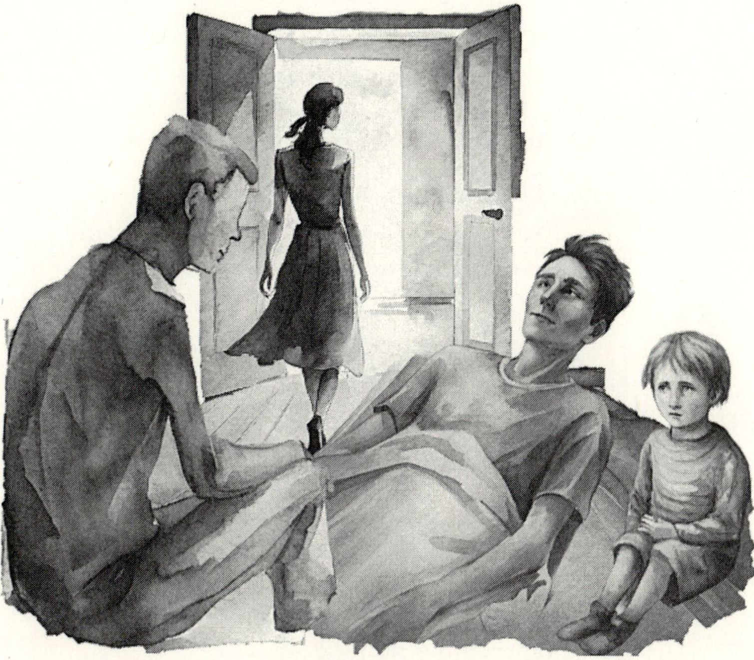

LADY DI

She is the epitome of beauty
emanating kindness,
Always bearing a sweet smile
illuminating the room
like a chandelier.

Unable to cope with the intense scrutiny,
she sobs and I reach out,
but she is moved away by the escorts.

She is in close proximity
And yet so far away.

Now as the fallen angel
lies lifeless
in the terribly mangled car,
Remorseful tears
roll down my cheeks,
for the enigmatic lady
I always knew
but never actually knew.

DEATH OR DISPATCH?

Why shall one be grieving over death?
For death is the most peaceful a time
that a man could possibly have.

Why shall one think
that death must be devastating?
This tranquil juncture
has a virtue of its own,
that no one can know,
except for the one
who lives through it.

This unknowable marvel
has the philosophers wondering
and the folks lamenting.
As Virginia in vain says;
"Death is the only experience I can't describe."

WHERE DO I BELONG?

Where do I belong?
Maybe in a mansion
of gothic architecture.
Ostentatious rooms with
pretty pictures adorning the walls,
Carpets worth a king's ransom
covering the mahogany floors.
But no,
This is not my home.

Where do I belong?
Maybe in a slum,
With rats and roaches running around,
With stinky and grimy alleys,
Surrounded by people
wearing soiled shirts,
With cries of horror and despair
filling the atmosphere.
But no,
This is not my home.

Where do I belong?
Perhaps in the Scottish outskirts,
Or in a tower
in the heart of the city.
Or maybe in an island
across the country.
But no,
That is not my home.
I belong, to myself.
I am my home.

CRUSH

She watches him
walking towards her
with chocolate croissants in his hands.
She smiles
as he passes her one,
taking a seat beside her.
As they both start to eat,
she takes a moment
to admire her best friend.
His dirty blonde mane
To his crimson cheeks,
Everything about him
was winsome to her.
Every now and then
he would grin widely at her,
revealing his pearly whites.
They talk about everything and nothing,
Sharing stupid jokes
and laughing together.

Now, it was twilight
And he was approached by his lover.
The boy stood up and walked up
to the nearby lamp post,
talking quietly with his partner.

She watches them in despair,
wishing to be his beloved.
She looks away,
overwhelmed with melancholy.
But just as she does,
his ocean blue eyes
gaze at her with such longing,
in hopes she'd turn back
and come into his arms.

GOODBYE, YOU

Sitting inside your car,
With you on the driver's seat,
Window glass glistening
with dew down trickling.
You turned up the heat,
The glass surface now foggy.

Outside,
it was pouring; chilly.
Inside,
with soft lights; cosy.

In a trice,
You tell me
of your forthcoming nuptial,
the word weighing down
heavily upon my heart.

Unable to forsake
this ephemeral but intimate affaire.
Times spent,
Talking,
Flirting,
Kissing,
Cuddling,
All seemingly evanescent,
now rushed through
my crestfallen mind.

You tell me
of your plans
to move abroad,
leaving me in the lurch.
I smile,
Veiling,
my state of woe,
and of despair and dolour.

Unable to relinquish
your mellow voice,
I listen to you talk,
About the future ahead,
With the ever-forlorn hope
of being a part of this chimera.

The rain,
lashing down now,
The pitter-patter of droplets
clattering on the windshield.
You look at me,
Bittersweet and lachrymose;
I look right back,
For once,
without the pall of false façade.
You grab my face
and lock your lips with mine
in a thrilling kiss,
Both lush and luscious.

We wallow a while in the warmth
of our embraced bodies.

Outside,
The rain,
now down to a drizzle.
It was time,
For me to bid you farewell,
For me to get out of this car,
Out of this bubble
and head homeward,
Back to myself.

THE UNFORGIVING MUSE

Life has been difficult.

In my pursuit of death,
I consider drowning myself
in the deep depths of the dark waters.
But I'm already drowning
in my sorrows
for what feels like forever,
Never quite reaching the bottom,
The anguish endlessly stifling me.

Just a slit on the sensitive skin
of my wrist would suffice.
But I'm already bleeding
from all the hurt
people have caused me,
Lacerating me of my forbearance
to all this abuse.
Yet, the bleeding never stops;
'tis ceaseless agony.

I consider poison.
But the pain of my broken heart
is already dissolving
the innermost contours of my psyche,
consuming me slowly but surely.

Remorseful retrospection
has become habitual
And pessimism a way of life,
But perpetual darkness had already
defeated my dying desire….
My melancholia has now become my muse.

DEATH BED

Austere, she stood
beside her father
lying stoically on his death bed.
He was unspeaking;
in too much agony
so as to utter a word.
His mind drifting
off to an abyss,
His memory slowly withering.

She ruminated remorsefully in retrospect
of their quarrels,
of heated arguments,
of constant bickering
and of the hurtful words
she had said for the mere sake
of trying to refute and rebut him.

With penitence,
she gently held his hand
and called for him
one last time.
He meekly opened his eyes
and smiled at her,
with all the dying embers
of his love for her.
A smile that said all,
One so genuine…
A smile that had her forgiven forevermore
and woefully the one she would see nevermore.

A EULOGY TO MY PUPPY

I remember,
The first time
I held you in my arms,
A wee ball of fluff and fur,
Eyes so soft and warm
With a tiny tongue
licking lovingly onto my face.

I remember,
Buying you toys,
all of your choice,
And a baby bed for you to sleep.
Yet, nothing brings you more joy
than to chew on my shoes
or to sleep on my bed,
cuddling up to me.

Years pass
and you grow big,
So does your love and trust;
Welcoming me always,
wagging that feathery tail of yours,
That coming back home
after a dull draining day,
feels infinitely more bearable.

My tears have not touched the ground
ever since I got you,
'cause you lick away
these salty signs of sorrow
and of misery and melancholy
right off my cheeks.

You never want to know
what has caused me such woe.
You never upbraid me
for any of my foibles.
You don't talk,
yet speak volumes
with your calming company
heartening me through my terrible ordeal.

You always answer when called,
adorably invading my personal space.
You show gratitude of the greatest kind,
A feature foreign to the folks of my kind.

You never lie,
Or pretend to like.
You love me all the same;
Even when I'm stinking with sweat
or when I'm at my worst.
You never judge,
or ever hold a grudge.
You love
selflessly, unconditionally and wholeheartedly.

After a decade,
of this benediction bestowed upon me,
the quietus has finally seized you,
away from me.

My tears touch the ground
under which you are buried,
My darling, precious pet
Resting peacefully,
safe and sound.

I hope in the Elysian fields,
You have plenty of places to play and prance around.
I shall hope
to see you again
My dearest friend,
at a rainbow's end.

CERTAINTIES

I hate certainties
I hate the certainty
of a mathematical equation.
I hate the certainty of the laws of physics.
I hate the certainty of Murphy's law;
"Anything that can go wrong will go wrong."
I hate the certainty that
I won't stop procrastinating.
I hate the certainty that
my preferences will change.
I hate the certainty
that nothing is forevermore.
I hate the certainty that anyone
can turn their backs on you.
I hate the certainty that
I'll cry if I laugh too much.
I hate the certainty that
I'll start to despise a person
if I like them too much.
I hate the certainty that
I'll never see my father again.
I hate the certainty of an event
transpiring which I dread the most.
I hate the certainty that
fantasy will always be kinder than reality.

I hate the certainty that
I'll lose people close to me.
I hate the certainty
that I'll grow old.
I hate the certainty
that I'll die alone.
I hate the certainty that
I'll lose my appetite
if I watch something nauseating.
I hate the certainty that
one day I'll be too sick
to write any more poems.
I hate the certainty of a promise,
especially a false one.
I hate the certainty that
I'll have to conclude this in some way;
And I'm certainly uncertain in that regard.

HIS LOVE

She looks up into the sky,
Gazing at the clouds,
It was beautiful, blissful.
So was his love.

How they change their forms,
Evincing all the enchanting emotions,
So did his love.

When it drizzles,
She steps out,
Wanting to feel a part of it.
And it showers it's love on her.
So did his love.

Now, she is standing
on the summit,
trying to reach for the clouds,
to feel them.
But it fades away
into nothingness.
It was cold and distant;
a sham.
So was his love.

THE NIGHTMARE

She hears a distant howl
of a wolf somewhere.
The mist hazing the dark forest,
Sounds of nocturnal creatures
filling her senses.
A perturbing whimper, getting closer.
She tries to move away
Yet still feeling herself in the vicinity
of the sordid soul.
A whispered greeting abreast.
Sending chills down her spine.
'twas like falling down
an abyss.

Opening her eyes, startled;
Nothing was amiss.
"Just a nightmare," she mused,
Drifting off
to a dreamless slumber.

But in the corner of her chamber,
There was a demon indeed
Waiting to pounce
on the sleeping girl.

LONELINESS

Loneliness is crooked devil;
I'm sitting in a bright room,
Yet I feel the darkness
looming above me.
For a moment,
flashes of a gloomy future crosses my mind,
And suddenly I'm reminded
of everything I've lost.
Fears and regrets creeping in,
The feeling of being alone ever powerful.
Slowly losing all hope,
That feeling of being unloved,
of not having someone
to keep me grounded;
it's all there
in the quiet of my mind.
I weep silently
as I close my eyes,
to drift off
to the lands of dreams.
To escape this black-hearted spectre.